Rugby football at Cambridge was challenged continu[a...]
codes … the arguments over football practices led to t[...]
Rules of 1863 on which the Football Association code[...]

Rugby [...]
Running With Th[e ...]
describing how [...]

To call a man an Oxford man is to pay him
the highest compliment that can be paid to
a human being.

The great Victorian statesman William Ewart Gladstone
(1809–98) on the value of his studies

Now for the beauty of Cambridge – the
beauty of beauties – King's College Chapel!

Novelist Maria Edgeworth (1767–1849) praising the most
famous building in Cambridge in 1813

I cannot let the bonnets in … they would occupy
the seats in mere disappointed puzzlement.

Oxford lecturer John Ruskin voices his prejudices
against woman scholars in 1871

*ABOVE: William Gladstone, who
attended Christ Church, Oxford.*

[I]t is often assumed that the Oxford-Cambridge rivalry is a shared Oxbridge joke to baffle the yokels
[o]utside. In fact, there are hostility and suspicion between the two places. Oxford fears and rejects the
[c]old, ruthless spirit of inquiry, the questioning of accepted ideas, of Cambridge. Cambridge mocks the
[l]iberal 'amateurism' of Oxford, and especially the many politicians it produces.

Birmingham Post literary editor Keith Brace describing
Oxford/Cambridge rivalry in 1986

TIMELINE

1167	The year often hailed as the birth of Oxford University after Henry II barred English students from the University of Paris.
1209	Cambridge University created when theologian Dr John Grim deserted Oxford with colleagues to return to his home town.
10 February 1355	Start of St Scholastica's Day Riot in Oxford, resulting in 63 student deaths.
1478	Oxford University Press, the world's largest university publisher, founded.
16 October 1555 & 21 March 1556	Oxford Martyrs, Hugh Latimer, Nicholas Ridley and Thomas Cranmer, burned at the stake.
22 January 1644	Charles I convenes The Oxford Parliament at Christ Church Hall during the Civil War.
4 April 1721	Former King's College, Cambridge student Robert Walpole becomes Britain's first 'prime minister'.
10 June 1829	First Oxford and Cambridge Boat Race held at Henley-on-Thames.
8 December 1863	The 1863 Cambridge Rules adapted by the Football Association heralding the birth of soccer.
October 1869	Girton College, Cambridge's first residential women's college, opens.
1879	Oxford's first women's colleges, Lady Margaret Hall and Somerville, open.
1920	Oxford awards degrees to women 28 years ahead of Cambridge.
14 April 1932	At Cambridge's Cavendish Laboratory, Ernest Rutherford's two scientists, Ernest Walton and John Cockcroft, first split the atom artificially in a completely controlled manner.
9 February 1933	The Oxford Union motion 'That this house will in no circumstances fight for king and country' approved by 275 to 153 votes.
28 February 1953	Cambridge scientists Francis Crick and James Watson discover the structure of DNA.
6 May 1954	Oxford's Roger Bannister breaks the fabled four-minute mile barrier at the university's Iffley Road track.
16 June 1988	Cambridge's Lucasian Professor of Mathematics, Professor Stephen Hawking, publishes his book *A Brief History of Time* which sells more than nine million copies.
28 March 2004	Cambridge wins the 150th Boat Race by six lengths after controversial clashing of oars, 175 years after the event was inaugurated.

OPPOSITE: View of All Souls College from St Mary's Tower, Oxford

THE GREAT RIVALS
Oxford versus Cambridge

Ross Reyburn

Oxford and Cambridge are the world's two most famous universities. Their origins date back to the Middle Ages, producing a stunning architectural legacy (Oxford has 197 and Cambridge 63 Grade I listed buildings) that, added to their riverside settings, provides two of Britain's most popular tourist destinations.

The Oxford and Cambridge University Boat Race is a national institution. Cambridge gave the world the rules of soccer, and between them the two universities have produced 32 England cricket captains and more than 600 rugby union internationals.

Less well-known are their often violent histories and the vast list of world-renowned achievements in the fields of literature, politics, science, religion and humour of those who studied here. In *The Great Rivals* we offer an unprecedented insight into the Oxford/Cambridge story, comparing their achievements and highlighting a memorable rivalry.

Two Shades of Blue
A Brief History of Oxford and Cambridge Universities

Never have two centres of learning produced such a fascinating combination of intellectual genius, academic achievement, sporting prowess, red-hot rivalry, scandal and violent uprising as the universities of Oxford and Cambridge. Their overall impact is immense and immeasurable. Their names and reputations are globally recognizable, maybe not so readily as the Christian crucifix or Macdonald's – but not far behind. They have illustrious histories stretching back hundreds of years – approaching a millennium in Oxford's case and 800 years for Cambridge – and boast prestigious alumni whose names read like a global *Who's Who*. Some of the most important scientific discoveries and advances happened in the laboratories and libraries here. Many of the world's most powerful and influential political leaders, humanists, writers, humourists and sports stars studied here. And they provide two of Britain's hottest tourist destinations with their wealth of magnificent historic buildings and beautiful riverside settings where punting is a favourite occupation.

Within easy reach of London, Oxford – the poet Matthew Arnold's 'sweet city with her dreaming spires' – has some nine million tourists a year. More remote Cambridge, where The Backs – the extensive rear gardens and grasslands of six colleges by the winding River Cam – offer one of the most charming of all city river landscapes, attracts over four million visitors annually. The Boat Race remains the ultimate symbol of the universities' rivalry as one of the world's most popular sporting contests. And the mere mention of 'the Dark Blues' or 'the Light Blues' reflected in their sports strips conveys Oxford or Cambridge to millions. Images of misty mornings on the River Cam and Oxford's ancient colleges imply havens of undisturbed intellectual tranquillity – but don't be deceived. Rarely have two centres of learning had such tarnished reputations, and yet the fighting, debauchery and mob rule are not found in any tours led by town guides.

No clear date exists for Oxford's foundation, but it is the oldest university in the English-speaking world; teaching in the town dates back to at least 1096 while its rapid development came after Henry II banned English students from attending the University of Paris in 1167. Ironically it was murder in Oxford that led to the creation of Cambridge University in 1209. Benedictine chronicler Roger of Wendover (died 1236) reported 'a certain clerk who was studying Arts at Oxford by chance slew a certain woman and finding that she was dead sought safety in flight'. The guilty party was not found but townsfolk hanged three clerks from his lodgings. The result was 'some 3,000 clerks, both masters and scholars, departed Oxford'. Among the deserters was influential

LEFT: Britain's most scenic punting location: The Backs, Cambridge.

theologian Dr John Grim, described by Pope Innocent III as 'Master of the schools of Oxford'. His return with colleagues to his home town is generally acknowledged as the birth of Cambridge University.

The Middle Ages saw many examples of mayhem and killings in 'town and gown' disputes and tribal conflicts between student factions. Oxford witnessed the most notorious of all 'town and gown' battles between townsfolk and students, the St Scholastica's Feast Day Riot. On 10 February 1355, at the Swyndlestock Tavern, scholars took offence at being served poor quality wine by the landlord, one John of Croydon, and threw a jug of the questionable drink at his head. Hordes of townsfolk, armed with bows and arrows, came to the landlord's aid and two days

BELOW: An artist's impression of a 'town and gown' battle in Oxford in 1845.

of violence followed with the scholars finally fleeing the city after 2,000 countrymen joined the rioting. In his *History and Antiquities of the University of Oxford* (1674) Anthony Wood wrote: 'The countrymen advanced crying "Slea, Slea … Havock, Havock … Smyt fast, give gode knocks." … Such scholars as they found in the said Halls or Inns they killed or maimed, or grievously wounded.' The terrible event was not forgotten, for every year afterwards the Mayor of Oxford and 63 citizens – one for each student killed in the riot – processed in penitence to St Mary's Church until the ceremony was finally abolished in 1825. Neither was Cambridge immune to this kind of mayhem: in 1261, a scuffle between northern and southern students escalated into a 'town and gown' battle resulting in 16 towns-men being tried and hanged; in 1381, townies destroyed the university's charter and records.

Student excesses weren't confined to violence. In 1507, the Bishop of Winchester, visiting Magdalen College, Oxford, reported: 'Stokes was unchaste with the wife of a tailor, Stokysley baptized a cat and practised witchcraft … Smyth kept a ferret in college, Lenard a sparrow-hawk, Parkyns a weasel.' In 1636 William Laud, Archbishop of Canterbury and Chancellor of Oxford University, compiled his Laudian Code banning students from betting, attending plays, watching bull and bear baiting, and visiting houses where 'harlots are kept or harboured'. The unhappy aspects of the Oxbridge story also featured, barring Catholics and women from the two establishments until the 19th century.

Considering the tidal wave of major figures Oxbridge has produced, it seems incongruous that either institution could be dismissed as dismal, yet in 1734 the poet Thomas Gray wrote of Cambridge's teaching elite: 'The masters of Colleges are twelve grey-hair'd

BELOW LEFT: Bicycles beside the river in Cambridge. Few British towns can match the bike population of Oxford and Cambridge.

ABOVE: The rule maker: Sir Anthony van Dyck's portrait of William Laud, Archbishop of Canterbury and Chancellor of Oxford University.

ABOVE: *Oxford students display their social graces in Robert Cruikshank's 1825 lithograph.*

Gentlefolks, who are mad with pride, the Fellows are sleepy, drunken, dull illiterate Things.' In 1796, Oxford fared no better for historian Edward Gibbon wrote: 'The greater part of the public professors have for these many years given up altogether even the pretence of teaching.'

The riots have long passed into history but human nature being what it is it would be unrealistic to expect these great universities to be devoid of controversy today. In 2002 the 'cash for places' scandal that led to the resignation of two Pembroke College dons showed that while Cambridge had achieved notoriety with its spies, the misdeeds of Oxford University were not entirely confined to the fiction of Colin Dexter's Inspector Morse stories.

But today Oxford and its great rival – dismissively referred to as 'The Other Place' – continue adding to their astonishing roll-calls of great achievers. And in conversations heard in office corridors or crowded bars, the remarks 'He's an Oxford man' or 'She went to Cambridge' still evoke the expectation, rightly or wrongly, that someone exceptional is being described.

ABOVE: *A medieval masterwork: Cambridge's awesome King's College Chapel fan-vaulted ceiling supported by 22 buttresses.*

IN THE NAME OF THE LORD
The Churchmen of Oxford and Cambridge

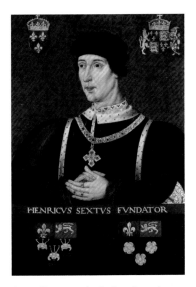

ABOVE: *The monarch who transformed Cambridge – Henry VI, founder of King's College.*

The great theologian John Wycliffe (*c*.1320–84) called Oxford 'The Vineyard of the Lord'. It is a description that suitably evokes the dominant role religion played in university life in the Middle Ages.

Oxford was run under ecclesiastical laws with many early colleges developing from the town's monastic houses. The grandest of all Oxford colleges, Christ Church, also known as Aedes Christi (House of Christ), even contains its own cathedral. Cambridge's early role was producing clergymen. Its emergence as a great university started with the patronage of Henry VI, appropriately highlighted by a magnificent architectural tribute to God's glory, King's College Chapel. While Henry VIII plundered the monasteries in the Reformation, he drew the line at interfering with Oxford and Cambridge declaring, 'I judge no land better bestowed than that which is given to our universities.'

However, many of the great churchmen and theological scholars produced by the two universities failed to survive turbulent ideological conflicts. Oxford's Wycliffe was denounced as a heretic for daring to challenge Catholic doctrines and even had his bones dug up after his death. The great humanist Sir Thomas More (1478–1535), who also studied at Oxford,

ABOVE: *King's College Choir singing at their Festival of Nine Lessons and Carols which has been broadcast worldwide since 1928.*

ABOVE LEFT: Joseph Kronheim's print from the late-19th century depicts Thomas Cranmer being burned at the stake in Oxford.

ABOVE RIGHT: Cardinal Thomas Wolsey, creator of Oxford's greatest college.

was executed on Tower Hill in London for not supporting Henry VIII's split with Rome. Originally Christ Church was created as Cardinal's College in 1524 by Cardinal Wolsey (*c*.1471–1530) but lost its former name when England's most powerful churchman was stripped of office by Henry VIII and died facing a treason charge. But the great Dutch humanist Erasmus of Rotterdam (*c*.1467–1536) remained unscathed from visiting Oxford and spending three years teaching in Cambridge.

Oxford's great Protestant reformer William Tyndale (*c*.1494–1536), responsible for the first direct translation of the Bible into English, was burned at the stake for heresy. And Cambridge's leading Reformation figures, Bishops Hugh Latimer (*c*.1485–1555), Nicholas Ridley (*c*.1500–55) and Archbishop of Canterbury Thomas Cranmer (1489–1556), became the Oxford Martyrs, being burned at the stake in their rival university town during Queen Mary's Catholic regime.

The Anglican hold on the two universities was demonstrated by the fact that in theory they banned Catholic students until Victorian times. However, in the 18th century Oxford did produce two famous non-conformists: John Wesley (1703–91) and his brother Charles (1707–88), founders of Methodism. In the next century the Oxford Movement – led by John Keble (1792–1866), Edward Pusey (1800–82) and John Henry Newman (1801–90) – campaigned for a return to High Church values. Later the charismatic Newman converted to Catholicism and deserted Oxford.

Today England's largely secular society is no longer dominated by the Church and neither are its two greatest universities. But Oxford remains a Christian university with its unique college cathedral, chapels and academic costumes, rituals and college names providing a permanent reminder of its deep religious heritage. And in Cambridge, King's College Chapel is the city's most celebrated building with a world-famous choir providing a Christmas Eve carols concert broadcast to many millions.

Since 1162, a total of 51 of the 64 Archbishops of Canterbury have studied at either Oxford (34) or Cambridge (17). In 1830, 408 of the 440 Church of England ordinations were Oxbridge graduates. In 1998, an estimated 18.7 per cent of those recommended for stipendiary training had Oxbridge degrees.

THE SCIENCE MASTERS
Evolution, Destruction and the Answer to Life

Sir Isaac Newton experimenting with light rays.

Modest he was not: Newton's sentiments were cloaked in ambiguity in a letter sent to his bitter rival Robert Hooke on 5 February 1676: 'What Des-Cartes did was a good step. You have added much several ways, and especially in taking ye colours of thin plates into philosophical consideration. If I have seen further it is by standing on the shoulders of giants.'

The medieval splendour of King's College Chapel and those fine Tudor college gatehouses hardly suggest a great centre of scientific discovery. But Cambridge scientists have given the world the laws of gravity, the forerunner to the computer, the Theory of Evolution, the foundation of nuclear fusion, the jet engine and DNA's double helix.

Arguably the world's greatest scientist Sir Isaac Newton (1643–1727) went to Trinity College aged 17. He later returned to Cambridge to spend some three decades as Lucasian Professor of Mathematics. During that time he produced his masterwork, *Philosophiae Naturalis Principia Mathematica* (1687), detailing the Laws of Gravity.

Ironically Charles Darwin (1809–82) arrived at Christ's College to study divinity in 1827. Later, his scientific voyage on HMS *Beagle* led to his ground-breaking Theory of Evolution in his book *On the Origin of Species* (1859), causing consternation in religious circles.

Cambridge justified its description as 'the Athens of Science' with two awesome scientific discoveries – the splitting of the atom in 1932 and the discovery of DNA's double helix in 1953 – at the university's famed Cavendish Laboratory. New Zealander Ernest Rutherford (1871–1937), the father of nuclear physics, studied at Cavendish in 1895 and returned as laboratory director in 1919, remaining there until he died 18 years later. In 1917, at Manchester University, he had produced the first artificial transformation of one element into another 'playing

RIGHT: The atom men: the great New Zealand physicist Lord Rutherford flanked by his team members Ernest Walton (left) and John Cockcroft after the duo split the atomic nucleus in Cambridge in April 1932.

marbles bombarding light atoms with alpha rays'. However, it wasn't until 1932, in Cambridge, that Rutherford's two scientists Ernest Walton (1903–95) and John Cockcroft (1897–1967) were the first to split the atomic nucleus artificially in a completely controlled manner.

While Lord Rutherford had pioneered the science that gave the world the benefits of nuclear energy and the horrors of the atomic bombs dropped on Hiroshima and Nagasaki, two other Cambridge scientists later discovered the molecular structure of DNA, heralding a new age in crime detection and medical advances – as well as the daunting future possibility of human cloning.

On 28 February 1953, Francis Crick (1916–2004) walked into the Eagle pub in Cambridge and announced: 'We have found the answer to life.' That morning the Northampton shoemaker's son and his American colleague James Watson (born 1928) had uncovered DNA's double helix. The pair owed a debt to two former Cambridge students: in London at King's College, Rosalind Franklin (1920–58) did key experimental work on DNA; fellow researcher Maurice Wilkins (1916–2004) showed Franklin's all important X-ray DNA diffraction picture to Watson. 'The instant I saw the picture my mouth fell open,' Watson recalled, as it 'gave several of the vital helical parameters.'

In 1962 the Nobel Prize was given to Watson, Crick and Wilkins – but not Franklin, who had died of cancer in 1958 when she was just 37.

Other major Cambridge scientists include: Charles Babbage (1791–1871), father of the computer; William Harvey (1578–1657), who discovered the circulation of blood; American

Above: James Watson (left) and Francis Crick with their DNA molecule model at Cambridge University's Cavendish Laboratory. Crick said: 'It's true that by blundering about we stumbled on gold, but the fact remains that we were looking for gold.'

Below left: Charles Darwin satirized as an ape on the front cover of The London Sketch Book, April 1874.

Below right: King's College, Cambridge, where a computer suite, the Turing Room, is named after the computer scientist Alan Turing, who studied here 1931–34.

ABOVE: The great scientist Stephen Hawking as a cox during his Oxford student days in 1961.

Katherine Blodgett (1898–1979), inventor of the first fully transparent glass; Sir Frank Whittle (1907–96), inventor of the jet engine; and the computer pioneer Alan Turing (1912–54), a key Engima code decipherer in the Second World War, who committed suicide after his homosexuality brought a court conviction.

Cambridge's stature as a world leader in science is highlighted by its 85 Nobel Prize winners, which compares to Oxford's 48. But Oxford's list of great scientists is also formidable.

In the remarkably versatile, irascible Robert Hooke (1635–1703), Oxford could lay claim to the 17th-century's greatest experimental scientist and a fitting rival to Cambridge's Newton. The father of microscopy, Hooke invented the universal joint, Hooke's law of elasticity and the iris diaphragm; he also coined the word 'cell' and was associated with numerous other inventions such as the balance spring. But an intense feud with Newton left him hugely underrated.

Modern planetary science owes much to Queen's College astronomers Edmond Halley (1656–1742), who gave his name to Halley's Comet, and American Rhodes Scholar Edwin Hubble (1889–1953), demonstrator of galaxies beyond the Milky Way. And Somerville College's Dorothy Hodgkin (1910–94) is regarded as one of the foremost X-ray crystallography scientists.

Finally, both universities can lay claim to the most celebrated of modern British scientists: Stephen Hawking. Born in Oxford in 1942, Hawking studied physics at University College in his home town. Despite suffering with motor neurone disease he proved a fitting successor to Newton as Cambridge University's Lucasian Professor of Mathematics (1979–2009), achieving worldwide recognition for his new insights into the Big Bang and black holes phenomena.

ABOVE: The Monocerotis star formation in the Milky Way pictured by the NASA Hubble Space Telescope, named in honour of the American astronomer who studied at Oxford.

SERVING THE NATION
Oxbridge Politicians, Mandarins and Other High Flyers

ABOVE: Cambridge's Robert Walpole, who was Britain's first prime minister from 1721 to 1742.

ABOVE: William Pitt the Younger, Britain's youngest prime minister, held office twice, in 1783–1801 and 1804–06.

No other universities can match the Oxbridge political legacy. In medieval times they were hugely influential when State and Church were the main power-brokers. And since the House of Commons became the main powerhouse of British politics, Oxbridge has provided an unceasing sequence of influential politicians.

Oxford had educated a total of 25 British prime ministers by the year 2000, including Sir Robert Peel, W.E. Gladstone, Clement Atlee, Harold Macmillan, Harold Wilson, Margaret Thatcher – the country's first female to hold the post – and Tony Blair. Christ Church alone has produced 13 prime ministers – only two fewer than Cambridge. Oxford's overseas politicians include American President Bill Clinton, India's first prime minister Jawaharlal Nehru, and the doomed trio: Nehru's daughter Indira Gandhi, India's first female prime minister (shot dead by two bodyguards in 1984), and Pakistani prime ministers Zulfikar Ali Bhutto (hanged in 1979) and his daughter Benazir Bhutto (assassinated in 2007). Nehru's political dynasty continued with Cambridge-educated Rajiv Gandhi, who succeeded his mother Indira at the age of 40 as India's youngest prime minister but was assassinated in 1991 by a suicide bomber.

In the 18th century, Cambridge could claim both Britain's first and youngest prime ministers in Robert Walpole and 24-year-old William Pitt. But Oxford's status as the main provider of Britain's leading politicians remains intact. No Cambridge man has been prime minister since Stanley Baldwin in 1937, while New Labour's Tony Blair in 1997 was the eighth Oxford premier since 1936, the year of Edward VIII's abdication. Most of the leading figures in the 2010 general election were Oxford graduates – Conservatives David Cameron, William Hague and Boris Johnson along with Labour's Lord Mandelson, the Miliband brothers (David and Ed) and Ed Balls – while Liberal Democrat leader Nick Clegg and deputy leader Vince Cable came from the 'The Other Place'.

The Oxbridge influence in the top strata of people running Britain is far from restricted to politics. When Church and Crown ruled England, Oxford and Cambridge provided the training ground for the nation's clergy (see pages 8–9). It is only since Victorian times that this dominance has ceased. And in that era,

the great imperialist Cecil Rhodes termed Oxford 'the energising source of Empire' and no less than 11 of the Viceroys and Governors General of India, England's greatest dominion, were products of the university's Christ Church.

While Oxford was known for its politicians, Cambridge has been described as the Mount Olympus of the natural sciences through its famed Cavendish Laboratory (see pages 10–12). Both universities have provided a large proportion of Britain's decision-makers among the countless numbers of Oxbridge civil servants, lawyers, financiers and media figures. The only major field with no great Oxbridge influence is the military; First World War flying ace Cyril 'Kid' Lowe, T.E. Lawrence (Lawrence of Arabia), the controversial Earl Haig and Lord Mountbatten proved exceptions, but the normal route to the services was through the military colleges. In the relatively recent past other universities have established high reputations in specialist fields. For example, the University of Birmingham Medical School in the 1980s achieved the unprecedented feat of producing the four Presidents of Royal Colleges holding office simultaneously.

The continued prestige of Britain's two oldest univerities has frequently led to criticisms of an Oxbridge bias in the world of work and selection elitism at the universities themselves. Historian David Starkey, discussing Cambridge's 800th anniversary in 2009 on the BBC Radio 4 *Today* programme, offered an interesting dismissal of those seeking a degree of social engineering of graduate intakes. Asked whether his former unversity was too elitist, Starkey replied: 'Can it be? … The question is silly. I was born in a council house and my mother scrubbed floors. All that does matter at Cambridge is talent wherever it comes from.'

Above: History in the making: Britain's first female prime minister Margaret Thatcher – a graduate of Somerville College, Oxford – outside No. 10 Downing Street after her 1979 general election victory.

'Cambridge has more Nobel laureates but Oxford has more prime ministers … Oxford people think they rule the world, whereas Cambridge people don't care who rules the world.'

German writer Peter Sager on how England's two greatest universities differ in *Oxford and Cambridge: An Uncommon History* (2005)

Right: Former American President Bill Clinton, a Rhodes scholarship student at University College, Oxford from 1968–70, on the Democratic campaign trail in Virginia in 2009.

The Language Masters
Writers, Poets and Lexicographers

ABOVE: John Milton, the great 17th-century poet and author.

BELOW: St John's College, Cambridge, where William Wordsworth graduated in 1791.

Myth or reality? 'Oxford for arts, Cambridge for sciences' was the 19th-century slogan. However, the comparison is not so clear-cut for both universities can claim an illustrious roll-call of writers and poets.

Oxford's famous literary figures – such as Dr Samuel Johnson, Percy Bysshe Shelley, Lewis Carroll, Oscar Wilde, Evelyn Waugh, T.S. Eliot, J.R.R. Tolkien and Sir John Betjeman – hardly outmatch a Cambridge frontline of, say, John Milton, Samuel Pepys, Lord Byron, William Makepeace Thackeray, William Wordsworth, E.M. Forster and Rupert Brooke.

Early examples of great Oxbridge poets were Oxford's John Donne (1572–1631), ever remembered for his lines 'No man is an island … Never send to know for whom the bell tolls; it tolls for thee', and Cambridge literary giant John Milton (1608–74), author of the epic poem *Paradise Lost*.

Two of England's two best-known literary sets also have strong links with Cambridge. Three great 'Romantic Poets' – Lord Byron (1788–1824; *Don Juan*), Samuel Taylor Coleridge (1772–1834; *The Rime of the Ancient Mariner*) and William Wordsworth (1770–1850; *The Prelude*) – studied here while a fourth, Percy Bysshe Shelley (1792–1822; *Prometheus Unbound*), managed to get sent down from Oxford.

In the early 1900s, Cambridge provided the spiritual home of the Bloomsbury Group, memorably described by one critic as 'a troupe of cultural dissidents and sexual vagabonds'. The father of Bloomsbury standard-bearer Virginia Woolf was a Cambridge man. Fellow Bloomsbury members – Virginia's brother Toby Stephens, her future husband Leonard Woolf as well as Lytton Strachey and Clive Bell – were all at Trinity College.

In 1854 Cambridge's Lord Alfred Tennyson wrote that most famous of Victorian martial poems, *The Charge of the Light Brigade*

ABOVE: Cambridge poets Ted Hughes and Sylvia Plath pictured in the early days of their ill-fated romance.

('All in the valley of Death/Rode the six hundred'). And in 1896, Cambridge classics lecturer A.E. Housman, who left Oxford without a degree, wrote *A Shropshire Lad*, his memorable poetic lament for doomed youth and 'the land of lost content'.

The universities have major literary links in both poetry and prose with the First World War. Sadly it was an Oxford man who was partly responsible for England's 'lost generation'; British commander General Sir Douglas Haig (Brasenose College, 1880–83) remained stubbornly committed to the murderous Western Front offensive despite 20,000 of his troops dying after their suicidal charge on German machine guns on that fateful first day of the Battle of the Somme, 1 July 1916.

The doom-ridden, poignant desolation of trench warfare was famously chronicled by two Great War poets who studied at Cambridge. Rupert Brooke (1887–1915), described by W.B. Yeats as 'the handsomest young man in England', died from a mosquito bite infection on his way to Gallipoli. Brooke's poem *The Soldier* (1914) contained those famously evocative lines: 'If I should die, think only this of me:/That there's some corner of a foreign field/That is for ever England.'

By contrast Captain Siegfried Sassoon (Clare College, Cambridge) survived the war, gained the Military Cross and produced anti-war poetry a world away from Brooke's idealism. *To a Citizen-Soldier* (1916) contained a harrowing reference to the Western Front battlefields: 'Where quit of time lies many a shining lad'. In *The General* (1918) he witheringly satirized the British leadership: '"He's a cheery old card," grunted Harry to Jack/As they slogged up to Arras with rifle and pack./But he did for them both by his plan of attack.'

Oxford graduates Robert Graves (who served alongside Sassoon) with *Goodbye To All That* (1929) and Vera Brittain, a war-time nurse, writing *Testament of Youth* (1933) produced memorable narrative accounts of the Western Front conflict. More recently

BELOW: Cambridge's famous First World War poets, the doomed Rupert Brooke (left) and the battle-scarred survivor Siegfried Sassoon, seen here in his army camp, alongside the harrowing, desolate Western Front battleground portrayed in their works.

'I must say the whole of Oxford has become *most* peculiar suddenly. Last night it was pullulating with women. You're to come away at once, out of danger': Sebastian Flyte's warning to Charles Ryder in Evelyn Waugh's *Brideshead Revisited*. In the award-winning 1980s TV drama series of the same name, the roles of Sebastian and Charles were played by Anthony Andrews (pictured above left) and Jeremy Irons (above right).

Cambridge novelist Sebastian Faulks provided a fictional tour de force on the horrors of the trenches with *Birdsong* (1994).

While Oxford laid claim to two 20th century poets, W.H. Auden and T.S. Eliot, Cambridge University was the setting that led to one of poetry's real-life tragedies: the doomed love affair between American poet Sylvia Plath and future Poet Laureate Ted Hughes that ended with her suicide in 1963.

Oxford has proved more prolific in terms of noteworthy fiction linked to the universities. In 1895 Thomas Hardy's *Jude The Obscure* – set in Christminster (Oxford) – caused outrage by questioning establishment and religious values, yet provided one of literature's most poignant tragedies through a fateful remark overheard by a child. Evelyn Waugh's *Brideshead Revisited*, published 50 years later, brilliantly evoked the disappearing world of hedonistic privilege enjoyed by the author in 1920s Oxford. His set included the remarkable Sir John Betjeman – grandmaster of light verse, preserver of England's architectural heritage and another future Poet Laureate. In recent decades the hugely popular television adaptation of Colin Dexter's Inspector Morse stories introduced the world of Oxford academia to many millions.

Oxford dons have also provided three of the most popular fictional works ever written. As Lewis Carroll the Revd Charles Dodgson, who spent most of his adult life at Christ Church, gave the world *Alice's Adventure in Wonderland* (1865). Ninety years later J.R.R. Tolkien produced Britain's most popular fantasy novel, *The Lord of the Rings* (1954–55), while his English department

colleague C.S. Lewis penned classic children's fantasy stories in *The Chronicles of Narnia* (1949–54).

Cambridge's literary repertoire includes the much-admired 20th-century novelist E.M. Forster (1879–1970) and earlier, in the 19th century, William Makepeace Thackeray (1811–63) who enjoyed a decadent five terms at Trinity College, leaving without a degree. Thackeray's masterwork *Vanity Fair* (1848) featuring Becky Sharp – social adventuress extraordinaire – satirized early 19th-century English society; the book was described by Oxford Emeritus Professor of English John Carey in 2001 as 'having strong claims to be the greatest novel in the English language' and 'the only English novel that challenges comparison with Tolstoy's *War and Peace*'.

However, Oxford can justify its higher literary reputation. In a *Sunday Times* article linked to his book *The Adventure of English* (2004) arts broadcaster Melvyn Bragg voiced the view: 'Oxford has a fair claim to being the home of the English language.' As evidence he cited the gold handle of a 'pointer' (for following a manuscript) belonging to Alfred the Great in the Ashmolean Museum, the fact that Pembroke scholar Dr Samuel Johnson wrote the first great English dictionary (1755), while Oxford University Press published the world-famous Oxford English Dictionary (1884–1928), the 'gatekeeper of the English language'. Bragg then added a quartet of Oxford scholars who influenced the way we speak: philosopher John Locke (1632–1704) for linguistic clarity; Lewis Carroll (1832–98), master of nonsense English; and the clerical scholars John Wycliffe (*c.*1320–84), early translator of the Bible into English, and William Tyndale (*c.*1494–1536), responsible for much of the magnificent language in the King James Bible.

But in recent decades both Oxford and Cambridge have retained their reputation as literary standard-bearers, while computer technology provides ever-increasing alternatives to conventional forms of language and communication.

'Let the jury consider their verdict,' the King said, for about the twentieth time that day.

'No, no!' said the Queen. 'Sentence first – verdict afterwards.'

'Stuff and nonsense!' said Alice loudly. 'The idea of having the sentence first!'

'Hold your tongue!' said the Queen, turning purple.

'I won't!' said Alice.

'Off with her head!' the Queen shouted at the top of her voice.

The Queen of Hearts gets her priorities right in Lewis Carroll's children's classic *Alice's Adventures in Wonderland* (1865)

A PLACE OF SOME SECRECY

The Cambridge Spies

ABOVE: Sir Francis Walsingham studied at King's College, Cambridge. As Elizabeth I's spymaster he oversaw the counter-plot which led to the execution in 1587 of her cousin, Mary Queen of Scots, for allegedly conspiring to take the Crown from Elizabeth.

BELOW: Haunt of spies: Trinity College, Cambridge.

Cambridge University can claim the dubious distinction of producing the most notorious spy ring in British history. Exposed but never caught, the 1930s Cambridge graduates Kim Philby (1912–88), Anthony Blunt (1907–83), Guy Burgess (1911–63) and Donald Maclean (1913–83) all met at Trinity College and were all to work as spies for the KGB, the Russian security, intelligence and secret police organization.

The somewhat clandestine atmosphere at Trinity where the famous Cambridge secret society The Apostles, with its homosexual ethos, met undoubtedly encouraged subversiveness. Burgess, Blunt and Maclean were all homosexuals and it was not until 1967 that sex between consenting adult males was decriminalized. Why would they choose to remain loyal to a country that imprisoned men for sleeping together?

To the Cambridge Four, as these men became known, Russia was a great social experiment, in contrast to class-ridden England, rather than a dangerous super power. The Four had enormous influence at the heart of the British establishment: the master gentleman spy Philby was head of M16's Soviet counter-intelligence operation; Burgess and Maclean both worked for the foreign service; Blunt was art advisor to HM Queen Elizabeth II.

They were far from the only figures passing information to the Soviets. In keeping with the Cambridge belief that everyone should have free access to knowledge, the Russian physicist

Pyotr Kapitsa in the Cavendish Laboratory passed nuclear research information back home. It was the confession of American Michael Straight (1916–2004), a Trinity Apostle and speechwriter for Franklin D. Roosevelt, that led to Blunt's exposure. And in 1990 a KGB defector named another Trinity man, John Cairncross (1913–95), as the Fifth Man in the Cambridge Spy Ring.

Alarmingly, the secrets Cambridge men passed to the Russians might have led to the ultimate horror: Germany acquiring the atomic bomb before the Allies, had not Hitler broken the Nazi-Soviet Pact and misguidedly invaded Russia in 1941.

Cambridge was also producing spies four centuries earlier: Sir Francis Walsingham (c.1532–90) was Elizabeth I's spymaster and both the murdered dramatist Christopher Marlowe (1564–93) and Queen's astrologer John Dee (1527–1608) were reputedly members of Walsingham's secret service. Dee signed his letters from the Continent '007' – the code name of another, more famous Cambridge-educated spy, writer Ian Fleming's fictional James Bond.

Oxford's spies have also been found in fiction rather than fact, notably in the novels of John le Carré and Graham Greene (a close friend of Kim Philby). But the Cambridge Spy Ring did have another Oxford link. After his 1963 defection to Moscow, Philby (posthumously honoured on a Soviet stamp) was supplied by KGB agents in Britain with his favourite Frank Cooper's Oxford Marmalade.

The great deceiver: the urbane Kim Philby is seen here successfully denying being a Soviet spy at a London press conference at his mother's Drayton Gardens home on 8 November 1955. In 1967 he offered this insight into his psyche: 'To betray you must first belong. I never belonged.'

SOMETHING COMPLETELY DIFFERENT
The Humourists of Oxford and Cambridge

ABOVE: The Beyond the Fringe *team in a 1964 adaptation of* A Trip to the Moon, *based on novels by Jules Verne and H.G. Wells.*

ABOVE: David Frost presenting That Was The Week That Was.

Humour may rarely change the world but in the free-spirited Swinging Sixties the 'Satire Boom' created by Oxbridge graduates did alter perceptions of British society. In the post-Suez Crisis years, with Britain no longer a world power, the establishment ceased to be immune from ridicule for its excesses.

It was two Oxford men, Edinburgh Festival director Robert Ponsonby and his assistant John Bassett, who launched the Satire Boom by combining former leading Cambridge Footlights players Peter Cook, a professional sketch writer, and Jonathan Miller, a junior doctor, along with the ex-Oxford Revue duo Dudley Moore, a jazz pianist, and historian Alan Bennett as the *Beyond the Fringe* revue for the 1960 festival. 'These four high priests of parody make most professional comedians look ham-handed and vulgar,' wrote *Daily Mail* critic Peter Lewis. The revue proved a huge hit not only in London but also on Broadway, even attracting a theatre visit from American president John F. Kennedy.

Television soon got in on the act with *That Was The Week That Was* (known as *TW3*) presented by 23-year-old Cambridge graduate David 'Hello, good evening and welcome' Frost. Labelled 'the bubonic plagiarist' by the *Beyond the Fringe* team, Frost achieved cult status in 1962–63 as *TW3* emptied pubs on Saturday evenings with viewing figures reaching 11 million.

An Oxbridge combination was also responsible for the creation of Britain's leading satirical magazine, *Private Eye*, in 1961. Under the editorship of co-founder Richard Ingrams, and since

Trinity College, Cambridge, where A.A. Milne (1882–1956) was a scholar. During his time there he edited the university's literary magazine *The Granta*, but will be eternally remembered for his stories that brought to life the childhood toys of his son, Christopher. Milne's *Winnie-the-Pooh* (1926) includes Owl being baffled by Rabbit:
'Hello, Rabbit, is that you?'
'Let's pretend it isn't and see what happens.'

ABOVE: *Oxford's wittiest literary figure, Oscar Wilde (1854–1900).*

'All right ... all right ... but apart from better sanitation and medicine and education and irrigation and public health and roads and a freshwater system and baths and public order ... what have the Romans done for us?'

Activist Reg, played by John Cleese, having difficulty denouncing the Romans in *Monty Python's Life of Brian*

1986 his successor Ian Hislop, it has been fearlessly attacking the misdeeds of everyone from politicians to celebrities.

Following the Satire Boom, the humourists of Oxford and Cambridge again joined forces producing the zany ground-breaking *Monty Python* television series (1969–74), living up to its catchphrase 'And now for something completely different'.

Cambridge graduates John Cleese, Eric Idle and Graham Chapman, Oxford men Michael Palin and Terry Jones plus American animator Terry Gilliam achieved huge popularity with absurdities such as The Dead Parrot Sketch, The Ministry of Silly Walks and *The Lumberjack Song*. The Python team also successfully produced films, notably their *Life of Brian* (1979), the story of Brian Cohen ('He's not the messiah – he's a very naughty boy!') who is mistaken for Jesus; the film ends with crucifixion victims singing *Always Look on the Bright Side of Life*.

Oxbridge humourists wrote their own scripts with satirist Peter Cook the acknowledged comic genius. His philosophizing as E.L. Wisty – 'Yes I could have been a judge but I never had the Latin for the judgin'' – and his squadron leader instructing his flight officer: 'I want you to lay down your life, Perkins ... we need a futile gesture at this stage. It will raise the whole tone of the war,' remain classic sketches. And John Cleese, co-writing the hugely successful television series *Fawlty Towers* (1975 and 1979) with his American first wife Connie Booth, produced what could well rank as the world's shortest joke when a hotel guest comes out with the classic remark: 'Pretentious? Moi?'

Cook and co proved the vanguard of a long succession of successful Oxbridge comedians and wits that later included Rowan Atkinson, Sacha Baron Cohen, Richard Curtis, Stephen Fry and Hugh Laurie. But long before the Satire Boom, Oxford's Christ Church don Charles Dodgson, writing as Lewis Carroll with his Alice in Wonderland adventures, and Cambridge graduate A.A. Milne's Winnie-the-Pooh stories provided classic children's literature with their whimsical humour. From Oxford's Magdalen College came the brilliant wit, Irish poet/playwright Oscar Wilde, and the poet John Betjeman, master of light verse with comic overtones who was appointed Poet Laureate in 1972.

Carroll, Milne, Wilde and Betjeman may not have matched the dramatic impact of the Oxbridge satirists, but they have achieved classic status in the English literary canon.

Think of what our Nation
  stands for,
Books from Boots' and
  country lanes,
Free speech, free passes,
  class distinction,
Democracy and proper drains.
Lord, put beneath Thy special care,
One-eighty-nine Cadogan Square.

Prayers from a lady concerned about her home surviving wartime bombing in John Betjeman's poem *In Westminster Abbey* (1940)

ABOVE: *Monty Python's John Cleese performs his Ministry of Silly Walks sketch.*

From Iffley Road to Everest
A Wondrous Sporting Legacy

ABOVE: 'I felt like an exploded light bulb.' As Roger Bannister breaks the four-minute mile barrier he provides one of Britain's most celebrated 20th-century sporting images.

A cinder running track for students is a humble setting for one of sport's greatest feats, but on 6 May 1954 Oxford University medical student Roger Bannister became the first man to break the fabled four-minute mile barrier at the university's Iffley Road track in 3 minutes 59.4 seconds. Aided by his two gifted pacemakers, fellow Oxford Blue Chris Chataway and Cambridge's Chris Brasher (future London Marathon founder), Bannister achieved sporting immortality as he was roared on 'by the faithful Oxford crowd'.

Oxford's role in this epic landmark can be backtracked to the great New Zealand athlete Jack Lovelock's world record 1,500 metres win in 3 minutes 47.8 seconds at the 1936 Berlin Olympics; like Bannister he had been an Exeter College student.

Cambridge's Olympic gold medallists have included Harold Abrahams (100 metres; Paris 1924), immortalized in the David Puttnam film *Chariots of Fire* (1981), and the flamboyant Lord Burghley (400 metres hurdles; Amsterdam 1928).

Oxford and Cambridge are credited with the birth of modern athletics on 5 March 1864, at Christ Church Ground, Oxford, when the first Oxford versus Cambridge athletics match was staged. But it is the Oxford v Cambridge rowing contest, known simply as The Boat Race, that became a national institution and the greatest example of Oxford/Cambridge rivalry.

Oxford won the first Boat Race at Henley-on-Thames in 1829, and in 1845 the race switched to the present 4¼ mile course along

BELOW: A British institution: the 2009 Boat Race, won by Oxford.

the River Thames from Putney to Mortlake. Cambridge head the victory count, though Oxford won a memorable race in near-gale conditions in 1987 under master coach Dan Topolski after their elite American crew members mutinied. Watched by some 250,000 people on the riverbank annually, the race's worldwide television audience has been estimated at beyond 100 million.

Oxford's C.B. Fry (1872–1956), the cricket and football international who equalled the world long jump record with a 23 feet 6½ inches leap in 1893, is ranked as Britain's greatest all-round sportsman of all time. However, in Liverpudlian Max Woosnam (1892–1965) Cambridge have their claimant to Fry's title. A scratch golfer, Woosnam captained Manchester City and England at football and, in California, leading the British Davis Cup team, found time to beat Charlie Chaplin at table tennis using a bread knife as a bat!

The two sports Oxford and Cambridge have most excelled at are cricket and rugby. The first Varsity match dates back to 1827 and by 1988 Oxbridge had produced 126 Test cricketers including 30 England captains. In 1878 Edward Lyttleton's famously unbeaten Cambridge inflicted an innings defeat on the touring Australians and routed Oxford with 19-year-old freshman A.G. Steel, rated second only to W.G. Grace in the late Victorian era, taking a record 13-73 in the Varsity match.

In C.B. Fry, along with Cambridge's Gilbert 'The Croucher' Jessop (1874–1955), the game's greatest hitter who 'wrecks the roofs of distant towns when set in his assault', and Prince Ranjitsinhji (1872–1933), master of the leg glance, Oxbridge fielded three gods of cricket's Edwardian Golden Era.

Above: A 1905 cover of Fry's The Outdoor Magazine, *edited by the great Edwardian sportsman C.B. Fry.*

'Everyone cares … the whole of London cares … every household … when I was a boy, great divisions in our household, the butler was Cambridge, the housemaid Oxford … I was Cambridge, nanny was violently Oxford … and so it goes on.'

Former Conservative Prime Minister Harold Macmillan highlighting the vast appeal of the Boat Race in a dreamy Edwardian reverie at the 1979 post-race banquet held at The Savoy Hotel in London

Left: Record setters: former Varsity match opponents Peter May (Cambridge) and Colin Cowdrey (Oxford) at the memorable match at Edgbaston in 1957.

Oxbridge England captains who recorded Ashes triumphs range from A.G. Steel, 'Plum' Warner, F.S. Jackson, Percy Chapman and 'Bodyline' mastermind Douglas Jardine to Peter May and Michael Brearley in the post-war era.

Edgbaston in 1957 offered the ultimate tribute to Oxbridge batting prowess when Cambridge graduate Peter May (285 not out) and his former Oxford rival Colin Cowdrey (154) scored their epic 411 partnership against the West Indies, Test cricket's highest fourth wicket stand.

Other celebrated Varsity cricketers include all-rounders Trevor Bailey and Imran Khan, the great New Zealand left-hander Martin Donnelly, double international M.J.K. Smith, regal Ted Dexter, Pakistan's Majid Khan, and Cambridge and England captain Michael Atherton who retired in 2001 after 115 Test appearances.

The increasing demands of the professional era geared to commercialism have signalled the death of the amateur. Oxbridge cricket and rugby is no longer able to compete in the top flight, but the fact that more than 600 rugby Blues gained international honours illustrates the huge debt the sport owes the two universities.

In 1872 the first Varsity rugby match was played at The Parks in Oxford, and university Blues played a crucial role in the England rugby's Golden Era from 1913–24 that included five Grand Slams. Oxford produced both Adrian Stoop, who famously revolutionized the art of backplay, and the most bewilderingly elusive of all England players – the legendary Ronnie Poulton (later Poulton-Palmer), killed by a sniper's bullet on the Western Front in 1915. From Cambridge came the

The greatest rugby feat by an Oxbridge student was that of Prince Alexander Obolensky, seen here scoring his legendary try against the 1936 New Zealanders at Twickenham. 'By what right do you presume to play for England?' asked the Prince of Wales before the game. 'I attend Oxford University, sir,' replied the 19-year-old Russian royal.

Left: Cambridge winger Chris Oti (far right). In December 1987 his two tries earned the Light Blues a 15–10 Varsity match win. Three months later Oti's stunning hat-trick led to a 35–3 demolition of Ireland at Twickenham, inspiring the crowd's rendition of Swing Low, Sweet Chariot, the African-American spiritual regularly sung in rugby clubhouses, which became England's unofficial rugby anthem. Sadly injuries halted Oti's route to greatness.

dashing flying ace C.N. 'Kid' Lowe, DFC, MC, who scored 18 wing tries in his 25 England wing appearances, and the dynamic back row forward Sir Wavell Wakefield who pioneered mobile forward play when forwards were regarded as 'little more than pushing machines'.

The Scotland 1925 Grand Slam side featured an entire Oxford three-quarter line including The Flying Scotsman Ian Smith, who scored four tries on successive Saturdays that season against France and then Wales. And on 4 January 1936 Oxford Russian student Prince Alexander Obolensky achieved rugby immortality shredding the New Zealand defence with an electrifying crossfield run to add to his earlier 40-yard try in England's decisive 13-0 win against the 1935–36 All Blacks.

ABOVE: *Soccer pioneers: a 2000 re-enactment of a Town v Gown football match at Parker's Piece remembers Cambridge's role in framing the rules of association football.*

In the post-war era, Oxbridge's talented internationals included England fly-halves Richard Sharp and Rob Andrew, the great Irish centre Mike Gibson, the electrifying Welsh runner Gerald Davies, Chris Oti, the dynamic Cambridge winger who won a Varsity match and destroyed Ireland in a memorable season, and Scotland and British Lions captain and full-back Gavin Hastings.

Unlike cricket and rugby union, Oxbridge soccer has had backwater status, but Cambridge has the proud distinction of providing the rules for the world's most popular sport. It was on Parker's Piece that Trinity College's H.C. Malden is credited with drawing up the first rules of football. In 1863 the Cambridge Rules were adapted by the Football Association, creating the game of soccer that was to become the world's most popular sport.

Finally, on the summit slopes of Mount Everest lie the bodies of Cambridge's brilliantly agile history graduate George Mallory and Oxford's athletic young rowing Blue Sandy Irvine. At 12.50 p.m. on 8 June 1924, expedition geologist Noel Odell spotted the pair 'moving with considerable alacrity' perhaps 800 feet (240 metres) and three hours from the summit. Did they climb the world's highest mountain before Hillary and Tenzing in 1953? In 1999, Mallory's alabaster-white body was found clinging to the North Face but where Irvine lies no one knows. If their Kodak camera is ever recovered, climbing's greatest mystery could be solved.

BELOW: *6 June 1924: the last photograph of mountaineers George Mallory (left) and Sandy Irvine alive, as they departed from the North Col for the summit of Mount Everest.*

Asked why he climbed Everest, Mallory is reported to have told a New York journalist, 'Because it is there.' These words convey the Corinthian spirit of the many legendary sportsmen who have worn the colours of Oxford and Cambridge.

HALLS OF FAME
A Selection of Leading Oxbridge Alumni

Oxford	Cambridge
Architects	
Sir Christopher Wren (1632–1723)	
Athletes	
Jack Lovelock (1910–49)	Harold Abrahams (1899–1978)
Sir Roger Bannister (born 1929)	Lord Burghley (1905–81)
Sir Christopher Chataway (born 1931)	Chris Brasher (1928–2003)
Broadcasters	
Sir Robin Day (1923–2000)	Alistair Cooke (1908–2004)
	Sir David Frost (born 1939)
Churchmen, Theologians and Humanists	
John Wycliffe (c.1320–84)	John Fisher (c.1469–1535)
Sir Thomas More (1478–1535)	Erasmus of Rotterdam (c.1467–1536)
Cardinal Wolsey (c.1471–1530)	Hugh Latimer (c.1485–1555)
William Tyndale (c.1494–1536)	Thomas Cranmer (1489–1556)
John Wesley (1703–91)	Nicholas Ridley (c.1500–55)
Charles Wesley (1707–88)	
John Henry Newman (1801–90)	
Cricketers	
Sir Pelham Warner (1873–1963)	A.G. Steel (1858–1914)
Douglas Jardine (1900–58)	F.S. Jackson (1870–1947)
Martin Donnelly (1917–99)	Prince Ranjitsinhji (1872–1933)
Sir Colin Cowdrey (1932–2000)	Gilbert Jessop (1874–1955)
M.J.K. Smith (born 1933)	P.B.H. May (1929–94)
Majid Khan (born 1946)	E. R. Dexter (born 1935)
	J.M. Brearley (born 1942)
	Michael Atherton (born 1968)
Diarists	
John Evelyn (1620–1706)	Samuel Pepys (1633–1703)
Economists	
William Beveridge (1879–1963)	John Maynard Keynes (1883–1946)
Humourists	
Richard Ingrams (born 1937)	Peter Cook (1937–95)
	John Cleese (born 1939)
Inventors	
Edmund Cartwright (1743–1823)	4th Earl of Sandwich (1718–92)
Bernard Bosanquet (1877–1936)	Sir Frank Whittle (1907–96)
	Sir Christopher Cockerell (1910–99)
Lexicographer	
Dr Samuel Johnson (1709-84)	
Military figures	
Sir Walter Raleigh (c.1552–1618)	Oliver Cromwell (1599–1658)
Earl Haig (1861–1928)	1st Baron Tedder (1890–1967)
T.E. Lawrence(1888–1935)	1st Earl Mountbatten of Burma (1900–79)
Mountaineers	
Sandy Irvine (1902–24)	George Mallory (1886–1924)

Philosophers

Thomas Hobbes (1588–1679)	Francis Bacon (1561–1626)
John Locke (1632–1704)	Bertrand Russell (1872–1970)
Adam Smith (1723–90)	Ludwig Wittgenstein (1889–1951)

Poets

John Donne (1572–1631)	John Dryden (1631–1700)
Percy Bysshe Shelley (1792–1822)	William Wordsworth (1770–1850)
Matthew Arnold (1822–88)	Samuel Taylor Coleridge (1772–1834)
A.E. Housman (1859–1936)	Lord Byron (1788–1824)
T.S. Eliot (1888–1965)	Lord Alfred Tennyson (1809–92)
Sir John Betjeman (1906–84)	Siegfried Sassoon (1886–1967)
W.H. Auden (1907–73)	Rupert Brooke (1887–1915)
Philip Larkin (1922–85)	Ted Hughes (1930–98)
Andrew Motion (born 1952)	Sylvia Plath (1932–63)

Politicians

Hugh Gaitskell (1906–63)	William Wilberforce (1759–1833)
Indira Gandhi (1917–84)	Jawaharlal Nehru (1889–1964)
Shirley Williams (born 1930)	Enoch Powell (1912–98)
Bill Clinton (born 1946)	Rajiv Gandhi (1944–91)
Benazir Bhutto (1953–2007)	

Prime Ministers

Earl of Wilmington (1673–1743)	Sir Robert Walpole (1676–1745)
Henry Pelham (1694–1754)	Duke of Newcastle (1693–1768)
Earl of Chatham (1708–78)	Charles Watson-Wentworth (1730–82)
George Grenville (1712–70)	
Lord North (1732–92)	Duke of Grafton (1735–1811)
Earl of Shelburne (1737–1805)	William Pitt the Younger (1759–1806)
Duke of Portland (1738–1809)	Spencer Perceval (1762–1812)
Henry Addington (1757–1844)	Robert Banks Jenkinson (1770–1828)
Lord Grenville (1759–1834)	Earl Grey (1764–1845)
George Canning (1770–1827)	Viscount Melbourne (1779–1848)
Earl of Liverpool (1770–1828)	Viscount Goderich (1782–1859)
Sir Robert Peel (1788–1850)	Earl of Aberdeen (1784–1860)
Earl of Derby (1799–1869)	Viscount Palmerston (1784–1865)
W.E. Gladstone (1809–98)	Sir Henry Campbell-Bannerman (1836–1908)
Marquess of Salisbury (1830–1903)	Arthur Balfour (1848–1930)
Earl of Rosebery (1847–1929)	Stanley Baldwin (1867–1947)
Herbert Henry Asquith (1852–1967)	
Clement Attlee (1883–1967)	
Harold Macmillan (1894–1986)	
Sir Anthony Eden (1897–1977)	
Sir Alec Douglas-Home (1903–95)	
Harold Wilson (1916–95)	
Edward Heath (1916–2005)	
Margaret Thatcher (born 1925)	
Tony Blair (born 1953)	

Rowers

Sir Matthew Pinsent (born 1970)

Rugby Union Players

Adrian Stoop (1883–1957)	C.N. Lowe (1891–1983)
Ronald Poulton-Palmer (1889–1915)	Sir Wavell Wakefield (1898-1983)
I.S. Smith (1903–72)	Wilf Wooller (1912–97)
Peter Cranmer (1914–94)	Cliff Jones (born 1914)
Prince Obolensky (1916–40)	Mike Gibson (born 1942)
Richard Sharp (born 1938)	Gavin Hastings (born 1962)
Chris Laidlaw (born 1943)	Rob Andrew (born 1963)
Gerald Davies (born 1945)	
David Kirk (born 1960)	

Scientists

Robert Hooke (1635–1703)	William Harvey (1578–1657)
Edmond Halley (1656–1742)	Sir Isaac Newton (1643–1727)
Edwin Hubble (1889–1953)	Charles Babbage (1791–1871)
Dorothy Hodgkin (1910–94)	Charles Darwin (1809–82)
Stephen Hawking (born 1942)	Sir Ernest Rutherford (1871–1937)
	Sir John Cockcroft (1897–1967)
	Katherine Blodgett (1898–1979)
	Ernest Walton (1903–95)
	Alan Turing (1912–54)
	Francis Crick (1916–2004)
	Maurice Wilkins (1916–2004)
	Rosalind Franklin (1920–58)
	James D. Watson (born 1928)
	Stephen Hawking (born 1942)

Spies

	John Dee (1527–1608)
	Sir Francis Walsingham (c.1532–90)
	Christopher Marlowe (1564–93)
	Anthony Blunt (1907–83)
	Guy Burgess (1911–63)
	Kim Philby (1912–88)
	Donald Maclean (1913–83)
	John Cairncross (1913–95)

Sport's Greatest All-Rounders

C.B. Fry (1872–1956)	Max Woosnam (1892–1965)

Writers

Jonathan Swift (1667–1745)	John Milton (1608–74)
Lewis Carroll (1832–98)	Laurence Sterne (1713–68)
Oscar Wilde (1854–1900)	William Makepeace Thackeray (1811–63)
J.R.R. Tolkien (1892–1973)	E.M. Forster (1879–1970)
Vera Brittain (1893–1970)	A.A. Milne (1882–1956)
Robert Graves (1895–1985)	Colin Dexter (born 1930)
C.S. Lewis (1898–1963)	
Evelyn Waugh (1903–66)	
Graham Greene (1904–91)	
John le Carré (born 1931)	

ACKNOWLEDGEMENTS
Text written by and © Ross Reyburn. The author has asserted his moral rights.

Edited by Gill Knappett; designed by Heather Robbins.
Picture research by Jan Kean. Photographs reproduced by kind permission of: Alamy; IFC/
8 (The Art Gallery Collection), 1cr, 22d (Classic Image), 5bl, 11bl (The Print Collector),
8b (Geoffrey Robinson), 10tl (North Wind Picture Archives), 10br, 16bl, 18br, 22bl
Pictorial Press Ltd), 12bl (Dennis Hallinan), 13bl, 16cb, 16/17b (The Art Archive), 14t
Tim Graham), 14br (Morgan Hill), 15tl (Lebrecht Music and Arts Photo Library), 19tl
Interfoto), 23tl (Mary Evans Picture Library), 24tr (Lordprice Collection); Bridgeman
Art Library: 5t, 6br, 7t, 13tl; Colorsport: 25bl; Getty Images: 24bl, 26tr (Popperfoto), BC
Topical Press Agency/Stringer); Neil Jinkerson (for Pitkin Publishing): FC bl & r, 3, 4,
5tl & bl, 11br, 15b, 21br; © Derek Langley 2010/darknessandlight.co.uk: 19b; Lebrecht
Photo Library: 22br (David Farrell); Peter Lofts: 20t all; Mary Evans Picture Library: 9tl;
Rex Features: 12t, 17tl, 21tl & bl; Pitkin Publishing: IFC/1, 2tr, 7b, 9tr, 17tr, 18tl; Press
Association: FC main & 23b (Rebecca Naden), 26br; Science Photo Library: 11tr; TopFoto:
20br; www.exetermcr.com: 2tl; Woodruff Library: 16tl. The publisher will be pleased to
rectify any omissions in future editions.
Quotes reproduced by kind permission of: p1 Keith Brace quote, Birmingham Post;
p1 Running With The Ball: The Birth of Rugby Football, reprinted by permission of
HarperCollins Publishers Ltd, © 1991 Jennifer Macrory; p11 © Francis Crick quote,
reprinted by permission of Basic Books, a member of Perseus Books Group; p14 from
Oxford & Cambridge: An Uncommon History by Peter Sager, © 2005 and permission of
Thames & Hudson Ltd, London; p16 from To a Citizen Soldier and The General by
Siegfried Sassoon, permission of Barbara Levy Literary Agent; p17 from Brideshead
Revisited: the Sacred & Profane Memories of Captain Charles Ryder by and © Evelyn Waugh
1945, permission of Penguin Books Ltd; p18 Melvyn Bragg quotes, permission of Sheil
Land Associates (The Adventure of England, published by Sceptre); p21 Peter Lewis quote,
Daily Mail; p21 from Winnie-the-Pooh by A.A. Milne, © and permission of Curtis Brown
Group Ltd; p22 Peter Cook quotes, permission of Lin Cook and Billy Marsh Associates;
p22 'In Westminster Abbey' from Collected Poems by John Betjeman (first published 1955),
reproduced by permission of John Murray (Publishers); p22 from Monty Python's Life of
Brian, © Python (Monty) Pictures Ltd.

Publication in this form © Pitkin Publishing 2010. No part of this publication may
be reproduced by any means without the permission of Pitkin Publishing and the
copyright holders. Printed in Great Britain. ISBN: 978-1-84165-307-5   1/10

BACK COVER: The Boat Race and teams in its centenary year, 1929.

'This was an important race … the first chance since 1863
that the number of Cambridge wins could equal that of their rivals.'
OXFORD AND CAMBRIDGE UNIVERSITY BOAT RACE CENTENARY, 1929

PITKIN

ISBN: 978-1-84165-307-5

9 781841 653075